ways
to have
a **great day**
@ work

Stephanie Goddard Davidson

Sourcebooks, Inc.
Naperville, IL

This publication is designed to provide accurate and
authoritative information in regard to the subject matter
covered. It is sold with the understanding that the publisher
is not engaged in rendering legal, accounting, or other
professional service. If legal advice or other expert assistance
is required, the services of a competent professional person
should be sought.

> —*From a Declaration of Principals jointly adopted by*
> *a committee of the American Bar Association and*
> *a Committee of Publishers and Associations.*

Published by Sourcebooks, Inc.
P.O. Box 372
Naperville, Illinois 60566
(630) 961-3900
FAX: (630) 961-2168

ISBN 1-887166-41-6

Printed and bound in the United States of America

10   9   8   7   6   5   4   3   2   1

To my husband Bill—who has given me a perfect life.

acknowledgments

I would like to thank my agent Sheree Bykofsky and my editor Deb Werksman, who both said "yes" and then worked hard to make this book happen.

I would also like to thank that part of the Universe that gives you an idea for a book; then stays close by while you write it; taps the right people on the shoulder to help you; effortlessly.

introduction

Are you having a bad day at work—again? Often, in the midst of all there is to do, and all the stresses of the workplace, it's hard to remember that you have some control, some power, over how your day goes.

This book provides you with simple tips and techniques for making positive changes in your current position. Whether you read straight through and work one technique per day, or whether you dip into the book as needed, you will find you can actually make an impact on your circumstances, and have a great day at work no matter what's happening.

Having spent many years counseling and training employees and managers who are unhappy in their jobs, I have based my entire career on showing others how to have a great day at work. I have personally and professionally read hundreds of books on business, interpersonal relations, and self-help. This extensive reading has influenced my approach to solving the problems that are common in the workplace. The training manuals that I have created have been used successfully by many Fortune 100 companies. My promise to you is, if you apply the suggestions in this book, you'll have a renewed sense of purpose in your job, and the tools to make every day a great day.

make a list

Reflect back to the time you accepted your position. What were the aspects of this job that were important to you then? Try to remember how excited you were about these.

Now list ten reasons why you still like your job. Keep this list where you will come across it occasionally. When you do come across it, stop what you are doing and read it.

2

set more than just goals

Write down five things you would really like to see happen to you this year. Make sure these cover physical, social, romantic, career, and spiritual areas.

File this list in a thirty-day file that you can refer to every month to check your progress.

3

get it out of the way

Do the things you dislike most about your job first. Then reward yourself by doing the things you like best about your job.

maximize your salary

Determine one thing you can do to make better use of your salary this year (e.g., start a 401K, increase the percentage you already contribute to your 401K, cut down by half how often you go out to eat).

If you are already on a solid financial path, or if you are known to be a little too frugal, now figure out one way you can also reward yourself financially each pay day. A special dinner, a massage, a new plant. Just make sure the money is spent on you.

do something healthy

5

Do one thing today that you consider "healthy." It may be skipping that mid-afternoon candy bar or taking a walk at lunch hour. Or maybe just fastening your seatbelt on the way home.

Whatever you choose, don't discount it as too easy or silly. You have just sent a message to your subconscious that you are valuable.

6

plan by relationships, not by the hour

Try planning today by the relationships that are most important to you, instead of by schedules or deadlines. Everything we do is really just a reflection of the relationships we have with others or with ourselves.

Schedule at least two of these relationships into your day.

listen up

Make a conscious effort today to listen more than you speak.

breathe

Notice your breathing all day. When you find that you have forgotten to do this, take three slow, deep, gentle breaths and start again.

9 learn something new

Decide that every person that you come in contact with today can teach you something. Be aware of this possibility and manage the conversation toward this outcome.

mend fences

Consider a relationship at work in which you are dissatisfied (we all have one). Schedule a conversation that will address the issue. Throughout this process, consider where you have some responsibility for the condition of this relationship.

do what you can

It's easy to see what's not possible. The hard part
is seeing what can be done. Is someone or something
holding you back? Turn your attention today to the
things you can control and do something about them.

12

let it all hang out

The next time you are really angry with a co-worker write a "rage" letter. Really let it all out. When you are done, make sure it is completely destroyed. You will feel better. If you don't, write another and another until you do.

13

share your knowledge

What are a couple of things you know you are good at in your job? Write these down. Now, think of a population in your company that would benefit from having this information.

Create an outline for a presentation, an informal training, or even just a brown bag lunch-and-learn. (Use hand-outs only as a last resort.) Don't worry about your presentation skills. You are the expert sharing this information. What you share is important, not how you share it.

Take full responsibility for planning the presentation and carrying it through, checking with your boss and anyone else in the company who may be interested.

treat yourself

Buy yourself flowers and keep them on your desk. Or, consider buying yourself the perfect writing instrument, a small fishbowl and fish, or a plant.

stay positive

Try to say nothing negative or judgmental all day.
You won't be able to do it, but try anyway.

16

be part of the solution

Take a look at areas of your job where there are problems, or there's something missing. Then, come up with realistic "fixes" for these. If you cannot come up with a solution, move on. Focusing on impossible goals wastes your energy and creates unnecessary stress.

Share your solutions with someone who can help you implement them. Even if nothing changes, you'll be seen as someone who is trying to affect the workplace constructively.

17

change the scenery

Take a few minutes to go to a different floor, a different bathroom, or some other area where you rarely visit. If you can, take a few minutes there to slow down, breathe, or just sit quietly.

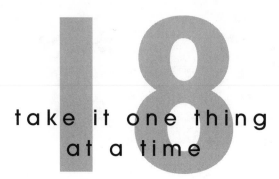

take it one thing
at a time

Concentrate on doing one thing at a time today. Stop multi-tasking. Notice how long it takes you to get your job done today versus the days you normally do more than one thing at the same time.

After you note that there is little difference in your productivity, take a look at your stress level at the end of the day.

pass the word

The next time someone goes above and beyond for you, tell that person's boss.

20

dress for success

If something you wear to work makes you feel too fat, too thin, too old, or just not your best—get rid of it. Even if you are on a tight wardrobe budget, it's not worth it. Your work is affected by your self-image.

You really only need five outfits. No one notices or cares how many outfits you own, just as long as you don't wear the same thing twice in a week.

21

find inspiration

Find a quote that really inspires you and post it somewhere prominent in your workspace. Even better, find a role model in your field, and read up on how he or she achieved success.

take it easy

If someone tells you that you are working too much, believe it, and consider slowing down.

build a bridge

If there is an employee, co-worker, or manager with whom you have some tension, take the first step and try to remedy it. Our success is only measured by the quality of our relationships.

The results we get at work are directly tied to this fundamental truth.

Any effort you make toward making the relationship better will not go unnoticed, even if it appears to at first.

notice your voice

Notice the quality and volume of your voice. Too soft? Too loud? Too high? Voice quality is a crucial part of how we communicate. Focus on how you use your voice today. Think of it as an instrument. When do you need to soft-pedal? When does increasing the volume help? When does it harm?

ask about motivation

If you have employees, ask them to list four or five things that really motivate them. This can be done in a staff meeting, via email, or one-on-one.

If you do not have employees, decide four or five things that really motivate you. Let your manager know what these are in a way that is positive and helpful. Approach this as a "group effort" to making the most of your contribution.

Most importantly, don't assume you know what motivates others or that they know what motivates you.

26 what's the problem?

You will get better results from thoroughly defining a problem before you try to solve it. The famous educator Thomas Dewey once said, "A problem well-defined is half solved." Don't jump into a solution. Focus on the problem or issue first. Make sure you have all the facts. Then, get down to the business of fixing it.

27

walk around

Walk around at a convenient time for you each day. Talk with the people that you need to before they find you. Make a regular practice of "managing by walking around." You'll have a lot more time for the things you need to do—more than you ever dreamed. People will feel your presence without the need to communicate through emails, unscheduled visits, or meetings.

sit and think

There is nothing wrong with taking time to just sit and think. Sometimes our society views sitting and thinking as being non-productive. Most Eastern cultures actually schedule parts of the day where they stop what they are doing and think.

In the words of author Sylvia Boorstein, "Don't just do something; sit there!"

give an award

Create some kind of gift or award for someone
you have been ignoring due to your workload. Make
sure you communicate the reason for the gift.

empower others

When someone comes to you with a problem, focus on empowering that person to come up with a solution. By being the problem-solver you end up taking responsibility for the outcome. Instead, let the person "own" the problem and the solution. You'll have more time for your own problems and will have encouraged a co-worker to work independently of you.

keep it work-related

The next time you feel you need to give someone criticism, decide on how this comment specifically relates to his or her performance. If it doesn't, you may be judging by style and how it differs from yours instead of a true work concern.

If it does relate to work, find a way to present it that focuses on the facts only, not on personality or style.

32 take responsibility

You are completely responsible for where you are in your career. To blame others is to give them your power. Instead, put that energy into taking the actions you need to get the job you want. Do at least one thing every day that gets you closer to that goal—no matter how small that action may seem.

love your work

Theodore Roosevelt said, "Far and away, the best prize that life offers is the chance to work hard at work worth doing."

Are you making career decisions based on money? Or title? Consider the words above. Money and title don't get you very far when you are miserable eight hours a day.

34

smile

Do you smile at work? If not, you may be confusing your serious look with professionalism. The reality is that not smiling just makes you appear unhappy.

35

read up!

Do you subscribe to any of your industry's or profession's publications? Even just browsing through these magazines, books, and newspapers will provide you with enough information to offer new and progressive ideas to your workplace. And others will start seeing you as someone who is leading, not following.

36

feedback takes two

When you feel you must give someone constructive feedback (and this will happen whether you manage others or not) remember to ask the person his or her opinion on the situation first.

The next step is to point out where you both have similar positions on the subject.

Only then give one or two suggestions that were not pointed out by the person (if there are any).

And, remember to balance your constructive feedback with some positive feedback as well.

37

give positive
reinforcement

If you want behaviors repeated by your co-workers, tell them specifically what you liked. Don't just say, "Good job." Tell them what the behavior was and why it was important to you.

This works for bosses, too!

38

trust yourself

Trust that you have everything you need inside of you to make a decision. Even if the decision is "wrong" later, you will learn from it. There are no bad decisions, only better ones.

you first!

The famous actress Katharine Hepburn said, "You learn in life that the only person you can really correct and change is yourself."

Consider at least three things at work that you are trying to change.

Now consider where you can modify your actions or thinking on these things.

thoughts are power

Steven Covey quotes in his bestselling *Seven Habits of Highly Effective People*, "Reap a thought, sow an action. Reap an action, sow a habit. Reap a habit, sow a lifetime."

Pay attention to your thoughts today. They create your life.

41

take ten!

The next time you can't get started on a task or project, tell yourself you will only work on it for ten minutes. Chances are you will stick with it once you've started, but even if you move on after ten minutes, you will have accomplished that much more.

42 let it go

List the things that are really bugging you at work. Create as many things as you can. Get specific. What about the color of the carpet? The copy machines? The tie your boss is wearing today?

Get out every drop of venom. Now go back and read the list. See where you can do something about any of these. Also see where you simply cannot and let it go. (And don't forget to notice that little smile on your face at some of the items.)

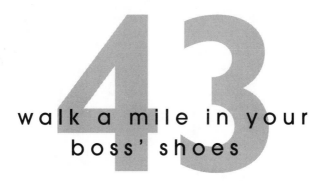

walk a mile in your boss' shoes

Sit quietly for a moment and imagine that you are your boss. Think about what his or her day is like, from the minute of arriving at the office to the walk outside at the end of the day. What might it be like to have those responsibilities, to work for his or her boss? Walk in your boss' shoes.

You will probably feel great relief that you have the job you do, and not the one your boss does!

44
reorganize

Can you reorganize your office space? Sometimes just changing your files around, moving your desk, or hanging pictures differently can make a big difference.

How about bringing in pictures, art, keepsakes, fragrant oils, even music? If conditions don't allow you to decorate, look at what you can do to make your workspace yours, even if you must keep your personal objects hidden in a drawer.

give a gift

Make today a day of giving gifts. Not presents, but gifts. Where can you help someone who is over-worked? Is someone due a compliment? Does the mailroom guy know that you notice the accuracy and consistency of the mail drop? Tell him.

Find some way to give a "gift" to every person with whom you come in contact today.

tune in

Stop what you are doing and notice your surroundings. Notice the chair you are sitting on (or how the floor feels if you are standing). Notice the color of the walls, the sounds you hear, the taste in your mouth. Try to sustain this awareness all day and see if your stress level goes down.

47

throw it out

Throw out any paperwork (with the exception of financial records) that has a date of two years or older, unless you absolutely can't part with it. If you feel this way about most items, consider that you may be holding onto unnecessary information. If it's something that important, you'll be able to get your hands on it again, even if you throw it out.

come up with win-win

Have you ever heard the term "win-win"? It's become a cultural icon. But what does it mean? Win-win means that there is always a better solution than compromise.

Start thinking in these terms. Instead of giving in or forcing your position on another, try coming up with a completely different solution. It's possible, but only if you try.

49

share your success strategies

Think about one or two things you do that contribute to your success and share them with someone else in an email, or tell someone about it over lunch. You'll be seen as someone who cares about other's success as well as your own—the true definition of a successful person.

no coincidences

The next time you are feeling unmotivated, try opening up this book to a random page. You'll probably find that you are reading exactly what you need right now.

51

lose track of time

What is one activity that you do that makes you lose all track of time? Everyone has at least one thing like this. Pay attention to this phenomenon. Once you find it, see how you can create a job or career around it.

take a look at your finances

How are your finances? Have you looked at your paycheck recently? I mean really looked at it? What deductions are you making, how much is going to taxes, where are you saving? Have you calculated the amount you pay in interest on your debt? Is it more than you have in stocks or savings?

Sit down today and get familiar with your finances. They won't improve without attention. True financial security is getting a handle on your money. Only then you can make wise career choices.

53

love your work

What do you love about your job? Is it more than what you hate about it? Can the things you love be turned into work? Start thinking about this today.

54

notice reactions

Watch how much you react to today. To react means to let other people, circumstances, or other externals control you. When you notice you are reacting, stop and try another way.

Even just noticing that you are about to react gives you a chance to respond with more power in the situation.

let it flow

When we try hard to do something, it is hard. When we just let things flow and roll with whatever comes our way, things start to work for us.

Try expending the least effort today (this doesn't mean doing nothing; that's much harder than going with the flow).

don't worry

Spending a lot of time feeling guilty or worrying?
Guilt is giving attention to something that has
past. Worry is spending time thinking about
something in the future. You don't have control
over either, so stop wasting your time and
increasing your stress.

Ask yourself what you can do right now about
the situation. And then do it. Your guilt or worry
will magically disappear.

57

create your future

What have you done to shape your future? If you haven't done much, it's time to get started. What do you want from your career?

Take small steps, but start making it happen today.

58 take a risk

We lose out on a lot in life when we play it safe.
Try being more courageous today. Even something
small like introducing yourself to someone you
have seen at work, but don't know, is a good step.
The day will only get better.

write a mission statement

If you do not have a mission statement, write one today. If you have one, get it out and review it. Make any changes to keep moving in the right direction.

A mission statement should have your long-term goals at the forefront. Career, love, physical health, spirituality, important relationships, and mental challenge are areas to address. Decide what you ultimately want to achieve in these areas and write it out.

This is your mission statement.

visualize

Always plan with the end result in mind. If you are giving a presentation to a group of experts or just filing that stack of papers on your desk, don't start anything until you have visualized what you want.

If you think this step isn't necessary, bear in mind that everything you do is a result of the mental picture you have of the end result. If you have a vague, half-hearted idea of what you want to accomplish, that is what you will get.

Be clear. Be specific.

go the extra mile

Give twice as much today as you normally do. Really go the extra mile. Instead of focusing on how much you have to do, or how little you get paid for it, give it all you've got just for today.

62

be of service

To be of service to others can be a path to happiness. Where can you be of service to the people you work with? Try looking at everything you do today as helping someone else instead of another checkmark on your "to do" list.

drink water

Keep a full glass of water or a water bottle nearby and drink at least 8 oz. of water each morning and afternoon, especially if you're in a climate-controlled building. You might find yourself lessening your tendencies toward junk food snacks, cigarette breaks, or nail-biting, and you might have more energy.

64 change your style

Try a completely different style today. If you are normally a "take charge" type, try emphasizing the part of you that can sit back and observe. If you normally hang in the background, assert your ideas today.

Each of us has elements of every personality type; we just rely on one style predominately. Break out of your usual way and develop the rest of you.

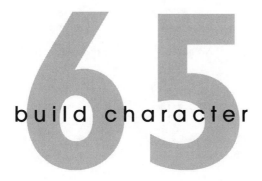

build character

Instead of developing your personality, charm, or intellect, try exercising your character today. Character is the root; personality the flower. Your external "beauty" is only as strong as the roots no one can see.

take the sting out

The next time you are upset and are responding via email or through some other written correspondence, file it away for awhile and get out of there! Eat, get a soda, splash cold water on your face or wrists. Then go back and read your message. Alter the "jabs" and harsh wording. Then send it.

work as a team

Management guru and author Harold Geneen says, "I don't believe in just ordering people to do things. You have to sort of grab an oar and row with them."

Even if you don't directly manage others, you must manage your results through others. The next time you are about to give instructions or demand something from another, consider where you will "grab an oar."

68

focus

While engaging in conversation today, focus on what the person is saying instead of formulating your reply.

You'll know what to say when it's your turn.

get to know others

If you are "low on the totem pole," start making plans to get to know the top executives in your company/workplace. Propose an idea or set up a meeting to get career guidance or advice on moving into something new.

If you are a top executive, schedule time to get to know the frontline employees in the workplace. Spend a day in roundtables or familiarizing yourself with someone's routine.

The knowledge and rewards of these actions will be unlimited.

renew

To be human is to be in constant renewal. We sleep to restore; we eat to re-energize; we shed cells daily to make room for new growth.

Follow your body's lead and renew your work today. Throw out unnecessary clutter, try completing your tasks in a whole new way, think of something you would like to try or be involved in and figure out how to get it.

71

value your opposite

Think of the person at work who is most different from you. Consider five positive traits about this individual. Open up to his or her contribution at work. If you draw a blank, get to know him or her better. Find what value this person provides.

72

follow your bliss

If money and education were no object, what would you be doing for a living? If it's not what you are doing now, start planning. Can you create aspects of this career in your current situation? Can you volunteer your time to a charity that works in this area?

How about taking just one course in this area or talking with those who are doing this work?

Life is short. Don't wait until later.

put values first

You may read and hear through "pop psychology" that feelings are the most important aspect of yourself and must be expressed. But often this behavior does not serve you well.

Put your values ahead of your feelings. The next time you are angry or worried or feeling guilty, think of the bigger issues to which you are committed, and act on these values, not on your feelings.

74

call people by their names

People respond in the deepest way to hearing their name. And one of the biggest insults is to forget a name or get someone's name wrong.

Use people's names today as often as you can. If you are bad with names, try a memory trick like "Claire has lots of hair." Or write down the name and a characteristic that stands out to you.

75

take a walk

If the weather is bad, walk your stairs or corridors. Purposely walk to achieve your tasks today. Avoid calling by phone or letting the mailroom handle it. As you walk, focus on each step.

76

be loyal to the absent

When you gossip, you are demonstrating that you are untrustworthy. This not only compromises your credibility but undermines your relationships. Your value as a co-worker will only multiply when you stop gossiping.

77

hail to the chief!

The next time you can find only fault with your boss, reflect on his or her credentials, education, personality strengths, or political savvy. There is at least one good reason why he or she is in charge.

If you can't find even one reason, you have to consider where you hold responsibility for this negative opinion.

78

downtime is
peaceful time

Use your "downtime" wisely. See it as a way to renew and recharge. Count your breaths or your blessings. Do this while standing in line or on a routine conference call. How about while watching TV or on the exercise bike? Use your time spent sitting in traffic as effective downtime.

79

find your balance

Find a balance in your life so that the time you spend at work is more enjoyable. Make a list of the areas in your life to which you must dedicate your time (career, family, social life, spirituality, solitude, volunteer work, etc.) and prioritize your list.

Compare your priorities to how you currently spend most of your time. On which activity do you spend the smallest amount of time? The largest? Does this correspond with what you find important?

This is the beginning point of finding balance in your life. You have to make choices. Decide how you will reconcile your two lists.

take it in

The next time you receive criticism or feedback
from someone about your work, consider these points:

- It's incredibly difficult to give someone feedback.
  The giver is more tense than you are.

- Without feedback, we never know what to
  change. It really is a gift.

- Recall feedback you have received in the past
  and recognize how valuable it eventually became.

  - Try to find the areas with which you and the
    giver agree.

    - People don't give feedback to be mean or
      judgmental. If they didn't care, they'd just
      let you fail.

81

sign up

Join a professional association. Find one that either suits your current profession or one into which you would like to move.

If you don't think you have the time, consider that you don't have to go to every meeting or become an officer. The pay-off is information, contacts, ideas, job prospects, suggestions for tackling difficult situations, and knowing you are improving.

This is time well spent.

82

reflect

Do you want to feel good about where you are today? Reflect on where you were five years ago.

 **83**

slow down

"We are what we repeatedly do. Excellence, then, is not an act, but a habit."

—Aristotle

Slow down today and choose excellence. Pay mindful attention to everything you do, say, think. Make all your results turn out the best you can, just for today.

84

just do it

You know that thing you have been putting off?
Stop right now and do it.

turn the tables

Try this today: when someone complains or is critical in some way, turn the conversation around and find the positive. Chances are this shift won't even be noticed, and you'll both walk away feeling better.

be a mentor

Find someone in your workplace you could help with improving a skill set or working through a problem. Here are some suggestions:

- Make a copy of a relevant magazine article.

- Share an announcement of a workshop.

- Have lunch and ask where a sympathetic ear would be helpful.

- Review that worrisome report; or be a mock audience for the big presentation.

- Teach him or her a software package you know.

87

admit your mistakes

You may think this is the wrong way to gain your co-workers respect, but in fact it is the best way.

play

We are all little kids in big bodies. Work is just the playground for grown-ups. Take the new guy to lunch. Invite someone who is sitting alone to sit with your group. Introduce yourself to someone you don't know. Tell a co-worker he or she is doing a great job.

89

attend to the basics

Don't deny your basic needs. Eat. Drink lots of water. Exercise. Get some air. Take time to rest. Go to bed early tonight. Don't let work dictate these things. Find ways to incorporate these necessary functions into even the busiest schedule.

90

look at the big picture

You will find very few policies and practices of your organization were implemented to make you unhappy. Try to see through the eyes of the whole organization.

91

try something different

Albert Einstein's definition of insanity is "to keep doing the same thing over and over again, expecting different results." If you're not getting the results you're after, why not try a different way?

92

a word of thanks

What has your boss done for you lately? How about saying "Thank you"? You may be delighted at the reaction.

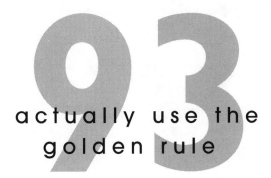

actually use the golden rule

Relationship building starts today! Try using the Golden Rule in building up a relationship with a co-worker. What is one step that person could take to make things better with you? Now go over and do that very thing.

countdown

Count your blessings. Don't stop until you find
at least ten.

just say no

Are you feeling overwhelmed? Are you able to confidently say "no" when you are being pushed?

Think of someone who recently told you it wasn't possible to do something you asked, or someone you would never dream of asking for a favor. Why do you think this is?

Chances are, this person knows how to set limits, and you respect that. If you set your limits and express yourself kindly and clearly, people won't view you as uncooperative, just in control of yourself. Try it and see!

reach out

Call that person you have been neglecting or want to get to know better and make plans to meet. Don't worry about being rejected, or that this is "too little, too late." Just do it. It will be appreciated.

97

don't get overworked

If your workload is surpassing your ability to handle it, ask your boss for advice on reprioritizing or managing the extra work.

You'll get one of two results:

1) some good ideas on getting organized or reshuffling things you had given too much importance; or

2) a lightening of your load, because the boss will have a full understanding of your commitments.

it takes two

Resist the incredible need to be right. Most of our conflict and tension in relationships stems from this mindset. Just for today, try opening up to others' way of seeing things. When you hear yourself defending your position, stop and consider the other side.

99

see your own strength

Find two things in this job where you have really shown remarkable power. Is it a specific skill? Handling a difficult person well? Meeting deadlines and being accurate? Realize this isn't luck. You have many strengths.

100

take a mental vacation

Reading is one of the best ways to take yourself out of your day-to-day world and escape for awhile. Go out and get that book you have been really wanting to read. No time? Try reading it during lunch, while standing in line, or a couple of pages before bed.

This doesn't work with trade journals or newspapers. Read a good book.

101

list your
accomplishments

Make a list of all the things you have accomplished in the past year. There are at least seven. Reflect on how productive you really have been, and how many great days you've had. Make today another one.

suggested reading

Boldt, Laurence. *Zen and the Art of Making a Living*. Arkana, 1993.

Bolten, Robert. *People Skills*. New York: Simon and Schuster, 1979.

Chopra, Deepak. *The Seven Laws of Spiritual Success*. New World Library, 1994.

Covey, Stephen, *The Seven Habits of Highly Effective People*. New York: Simon and Schuster, 1989.

Dyer, Wayne. *Your Erroneous Zones*. New York: Harper, 1976.

—. *You'll See It When You Believe It*. Avon, 1989.

Kabat-Zinn, Jon. *Wherever You Go, There You Are.* Hyperion, 1994.

Peale, Norman Vincent. *The Power of Positive Thinking.* Prentice Hall, 1956.

about the
author

Stephanie Goddard Davidson specializes in communication and interpersonal skills training and is CEO of Workforce Management Solutions, Inc., and Call Center Solutions, which provide management and employee development programs for such nationally recognized companies as MCI, BellSouth, Nextel and Rollins Protective Services.

She is also a nationally certified trainer for Covey's *Seven Habits of Highly Effective People*, Ridge's *People Skills for Managers and Individual Contributors*, and master certified in Zenger Miller's Management Programs; as well as an instructor with the American Management Association. Visit her Web site at http://www.callctrsolutions.com.

A portion of the proceeds from the sale of this book will go to organizations that assist economically disadvantaged women to enter the workforce.